Creative
Ministry
Bulletin
Boards

Summer

LEGACY PRESS®

Creative Ministry Bulletin Boards

Summer

Cindy Schooler

To my "long distance" friends who have kept our friendship alive through the years. Thanks to Lloyd and Phyllis, Tom and Sherry, Van, Flora, Anna and Mary.

CREATIVE MINISTRY BULLETIN BOARDS FOR SUMMER
©2007 by Legacy Press, fifth printing
ISBN 10: 1-885358-94-6
ISBN 13: 978-1-885358-94-3
Legacy reorder# LP46974
RELIGION / Christian Ministry / Children

Legacy Press
P.O. Box 261129
San Diego, CA 92196

Cover Illustrator: Renee Reichert
Interior Illustrator: Robin Olimb

Scriptures are from the *Holy Bible: New International Version* (North American Edition), ©1973, 1978, 1984 by the International Bible Society. Used by permission of Zondervan Bible Publishers.

Printed in the United States of America

CONTENTS

INTRODUCTION

Congratulations! You have the privilege of creating your church's bulletin boards!

Yes, bulletin boards can be a privilege. While they might take some extra energy and time to construct, bulletin boards are a valuable ministry tool. Bulletin boards can be used to instruct, explain, award and announce. So whether your church is planning an outreach or your members just need a little extra encouragement, you can provide a lively, attractive display that will meet their needs.

Creative Ministry Bulletin Boards offers everyone from the bulletin board rookie to the pro new concepts and ideas to ease the process. These boards have been tried and tested on the author's home church to gauge their responses and fine tune the bulletin board. The boards presented in this series are those in which her parishioners found the most benefit.

Even more exciting than the actual bulletin boards are the fellowship ideas included with each set of instructions. Talk with your church's pastor or Christian education director about how to incorporate these activities into the overall ministry plan of your church. Feel free to change the boards to suit your congregation's needs or personality.

Let God guide you as you minister to His people through this form of communication. Allow this Scripture be your prayer as you work for Him:

> *May the favor of the Lord our God rest upon us; establish the work of our hands for us*
> *— yes, establish the work of our hands.*
> Psalm 90:17

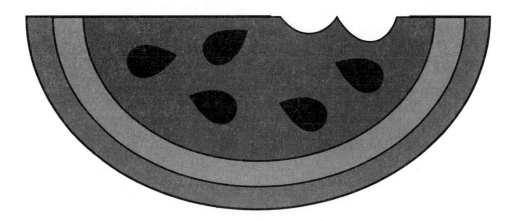

HOW TO CREATE BEAUTIFUL BULLETIN BOARDS

Each of the 15 ministry bulletin boards in this book contains complete instructions, patterns, lettering and borders to put the bulletin board together, plus related fellowship ideas for your congregation. The following pages will offer you ideas for your bulletin boards and explain how to best use the book.

If you are a "committee of one" responsible for bulletin boards at your church, consider recruiting older children or youth to help you. Most teens particularly enjoy coloring and cutting out materials, and even younger children can help with simple tasks. Not only will their assistance make your job easier, the young people will gain a greater appreciation for their place in the congregation when they see their work on the boards. Almost all of the boards require just scissors and a few other easy-to-obtain items. A list of materials is included with each board.

➤ BACKGROUNDS

Each bulletin board in this book includes suggestions for background colors. Most people use poster paper or construction paper. For efficiency, consider selecting a background color that will complement board designs you will be using throughout the season. Also, feel free to experiment with materials of your choice to add background interest, such as:

- textured fabrics: felt, flannel, burlap, fur, cheesecloth
- paper or plastic tablecloths
- gift wrap
- cotton batting
- newspapers
- brown paper bags crumpled and then flattened
- maps
- crepe paper
- colored tissue paper
- wallpaper
- self-stick plastic in colors or patterns
- shelf paper
- colorful corrugated paper available from school supply stores
- poster board on which figures may be permanently attached

➤ MAKING BULLETIN BOARDS THREE-DIMENSIONAL

Although bulletin boards are normally flat, there are many imaginative ways to add a three-dimensional effect to them. Some you may want to try:

- Place cork, cardboard or foam behind figures or letters.
- Attach large figures to the bulletin board by curving them slightly outward from the board.
- Glue or attach three-dimensional objects such as cotton balls, pieces of wood, twigs, nature items, feathers, yarn, toys, small clothing objects (like scarves and mittens), balloons, artificial flowers or leaves, chenille wire, fabrics, corrugated paper, sandpaper, crumpled aluminum foil or grocery bags, rope, plastic drinking straws — the list can go on and on!
- "Stuff" figures by putting crumpled newspaper or paper towels behind the figures before attaching them to the bulletin board.
- Flowers may be made from individual egg carton sections by cutting off the sections and painting, coloring or decorating them as desired.

- Heavy objects may be mounted in the following way: Cut two or more strips of bias binding tape or ribbon (available from fabric stores). Securely staple one end of the bias tape to the bulletin board, place it around the item to be mounted and then staple the other end (above the object) to the bulletin board so the object hangs securely on the bias tape strips.

➣ LETTERING

This book includes full-size lettering which is intended to be used on the bulletin boards that you create. To use the lettering, you may do the following:

- Trace the lettering onto colored construction paper, cut out each letter and mount them individually on the bulletin board.
- Duplicate the lettering onto any paper. Then place that page over the sheet of paper out of which you want to cut the letters. Cut through both sheets using scissors or a craft knife. Mount the letters individually on the bulletin board.
- Duplicate the lettering onto white paper and color in the letters with markers.
- Duplicate the lettering onto white or colored paper. Cut the words apart and mount each word on the bulletin board in strip form.
- Trace the lettering onto paper of any color using colored markers. Cut out the individual letters or cut apart the words and use them in strip form.
- Cut the individual letters out of two colors of paper at once. When mounting the letters on the bulletin board, lay one color on top of the other and offset the bottom letter slightly so it creates a shadow effect.
- Attractive lettering can also be made by cutting letters out of wallpaper, fabric, felt, colored or patterned self-stick plastic, gift wrap, grocery bags, newspapers and other materials. For a professional look, outline letters with a dark marker for a neat edge and good contrast. Always try to use dark colors for lettering, unless the background requires a contrasting color.
- Textures may be used for lettering also, either by cutting the letters out of textured materials or by gluing on glitter, sequins, straw, twigs, yarn, rope, lace, craft sticks, chenille wire or other materials.
- To mount the letters flat, staple them to the board, use double-sided tape or roll a small piece of tape to make it double-sided. Always put the tape under the letter so it does not show.
- Stagger the letters, arch them, dip them or make them look like stair steps or a wave by variegating one letter up and one letter down. Be a non-conformist when it comes to letter placement! Curve your lettering around the board, place your title down one side or across the bottom. Your title doesn't always have to be across the top of the bulletin board.

➣ DUPLICATING PATTERNS AND LETTERING

All patterns, lettering and borders in this book may be used right out of the book or traced, enlarged, reduced, duplicated or photocopied to create your bulletin board. Depending on the size of your board, you should enlarge the patterns so they adequately fill the space.

The easiest way to duplicate the materials in this book is to use a copy machine to simply copy the patterns, lettering or borders onto white or colored copy machine paper. For a nominal price you can copy onto colored paper at most copy centers. Construction paper works well in some copy machines.

You may also trace the materials in this book onto white or colored paper by holding the page you wish to trace up to a window or by using carbon paper.

Another way to enlarge items is with an overhead projector. Trace the items you wish to enlarge onto a transparency sheet, then project the image onto a sheet of paper attached to a wall. Adjust the projector until the image is the size you desire and trace the image onto the paper.

➣ MOUNTING MATERIALS ONTO YOUR BULLETIN BOARD

It is important that all materials stay securely on your bulletin board until you wish to take them down. The instructions in this book assume that you will staple most materials right to the board. Stapling materials directly to the bulletin board is the most secure method of mounting most materials and the staples are virtually unnoticeable. Be sure to have a staple remover handy both when you are creating the board and when you are taking it down. (Staples are much better for bulletin boards where small children circulate because it is quite difficult to pull a staple out of a bulletin board, unlike push pins and tacks.) Make certain that no loose staples are left on the floor after you finish working on the bulletin board. Pins may be used if you wish to support the materials rather than make holes. Double-sided tape, or tape rolled to make it double-sided, is also effective. For heavier materials, use carpet tape or packing tape.

➣ REUSING YOUR BULLETIN BOARDS

Cover both sides of your bulletin board figures with self-stick plastic. Cut around the figures, leaving a $1/4$" edge of plastic. (If one figure consists of several parts, put the parts together before covering them with plastic.) You may also glue figures to colored construction paper and cut around them, leaving a narrow border of construction paper. Also laminate the captions and borders to use again.

You will invest several hours in your bulletin board displays. Why not take some extra time to properly store your bulletin board patterns? Safe storage will save you hours of work in the future. Here are some hints for storing your completed bulletin boards:

• Take a picture of the completed board for future color references and diagrams.

• Attach the picture to the front of a large brown clasp envelope.

• Place completed patterns from bulletin boards in the envelope. Laminated patterns are easier to store and reuse.

• Use a black marker or pen to write the month or event for which you used the bulletin board in the upper right-hand corner of the envelope.

• Store the envelope in a filing cabinet or box until you are ready to reuse the bulletin board.

➣ VISITORS

Be sure to include extras for visitors when boards call for items for members to use or take. Your church's visitors will feel more welcome if they know you are prepared for them.

FORMAT OF THE BOOK

Each bulletin board's instructions are user-friendly. Look for the following sections in each set of instructions:

➤ SUGGESTED USAGE

Explains for which season or event the board is intended

➤ OBJECTIVE

A specific biblical issue the board is designed to address

➤ WHAT YOU NEED

A detailed description of all of the materials you will need to create the bulletin board

➤ WHAT TO DO

Step-by-step instructions to help you construct the bulletin board as it is shown in the illustration. Suggested lettering colors and borders are included.

➤ FELLOWSHIP

Each bulletin board includes an activity idea to encourage the congregation to interact with the board. The activity may be as simple as asking people to write their names on materials that are posted on the board. More significant fellowship ideas might suggest planning a special service at your church. Whatever the plan, these ideas were developed to help your congregation grow together as a family. The bulletin board you create will become a vital tool in the overall ministry of the church. It is an exciting new concept that will enrich the life of your church and its members!

BORDERS

Borders are the frame of your bulletin board. Just as you carefully choose an appropriate frame for a picture on the wall, you should choose a border that will enhance your bulletin board. Several border patterns are provided on the following pages for use with selected bulletin boards in this book. Many of them are essential in developing the fellowship ideas listed with each board.

The easiest method for creating and duplicating borders is described below. Simply measure the top, bottom and sides of your board (write down the measurements so you will have them the next time you are making a border). Then follow the directions for instant borders. Cut, fold and trace as many strips as you need for your board based on your measurements. You may use colored paper for the borders or copy the patterns onto white paper and color them in with markers.

Some of the borders are for individual use and should not be connected. To create these borders, measure the diameter of the bulletin board then copy or trace the border pattern onto white paper as an original guide. Cut construction paper into squares large enough for the white pattern to fit on. Place three or four squares together with the white pattern on top. Carefully cut along the outside line and repeat. Create enough borders to fit your bulletin board measurements.

Glue or tape the border lengths together. Use double-faced tape to attach the border directly to the frame, or staple the border to the edge of the bulletin board. Roll the border to store for future use.

Attractive borders may also be made with the following materials:
• artificial flowers, leaves or nature items
• rope or twine
• braided yarn
• wide gift wrap ribbon
• corrugated borders from school supply stores
• twisted crepe paper streamers
• Christmas tree garland
• aluminum foil

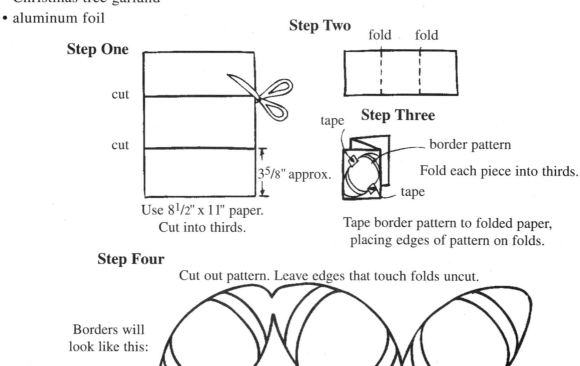

Step One

cut

cut

3⁵/₈" approx.

Use 8¹/₂" x 11" paper.
Cut into thirds.

Step Two

fold   fold

tape

Step Three

border pattern

Fold each piece into thirds.

tape

Tape border pattern to folded paper,
placing edges of pattern on folds.

Step Four

Cut out pattern. Leave edges that touch folds uncut.

Borders will
look like this:

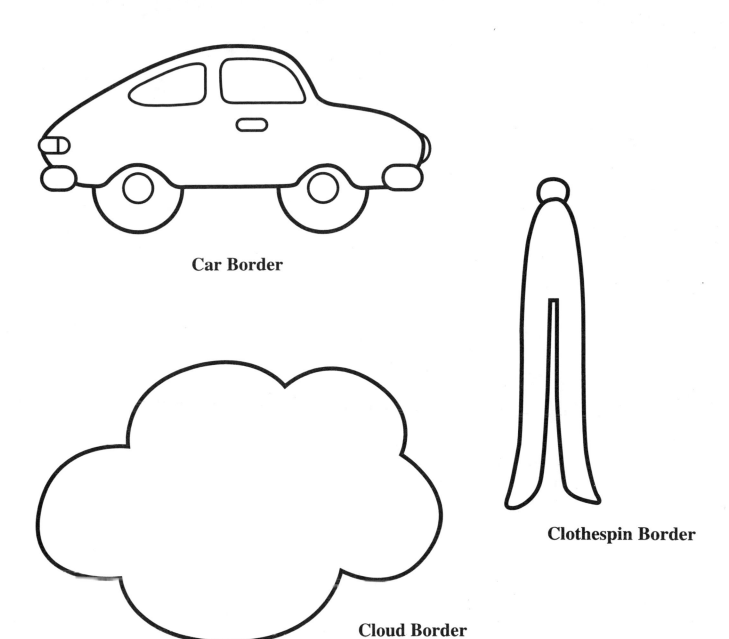

Car Border

Clothespin Border

Cloud Border

Money Border

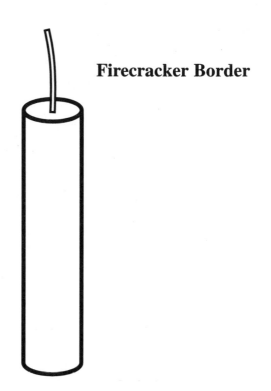 **Firecracker Border**

 **Ice Cream Cone Border**

Shell Border

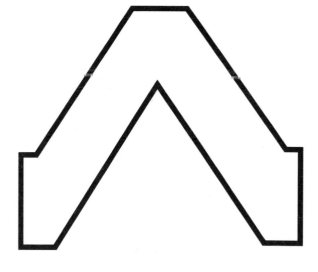

Geometric Border

Shoe Border

Thermometer Border

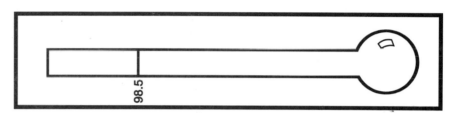

98.5

Volleyball Border

Wave Border

Let Jesus Be Your Light

Suggested Usage: **Graduation Day**

➤ OBJECTIVE
To promote Jesus' guidance

➤ WHAT YOU NEED
- gray, black and brown poster paper
- black and yellow construction paper
- flashlight pattern from page 24
- white or yellow chalk
- pencil
- black marker
- lettering from pages 25-26

➤ WHAT TO DO
1. Attach the black poster paper to the full bulletin board. There will be no border for this board.
2. Attach brown poster paper over the black paper on the bottom of the board, approximately 1/5 of the way up.
3. Minimally attach gray paper completely over the top 4/5 of the black paper (perhaps just stapling in the corners).
4. With a pencil, draw a tunnel opening shape on the gray paper.
5. Cut along the line and remove the gray paper to reveal the black tunnel.
6. Draw lines on the gray paper with a black marker to make it look like stones.
7. Copy the flashlight on yellow paper. Attach it to the black center of the tunnel. Draw rays from the flashlight with chalk.
8. Duplicate the lettering on black paper, cut it out and attach it to the board as shown.

➤ FELLOWSHIP
Use this bulletin board to celebrate a graduation day. Whether students are graduating from high school or college, or your church is graduating children within Sunday school, the church should recognize these important accomplishments. Ask the pastor to mention the graduates by name during the service and consider presenting a gift to each, such as a Bible. At a cake and punch celebration following the service, have several older adults share wisdom for life, both serious and humorous.

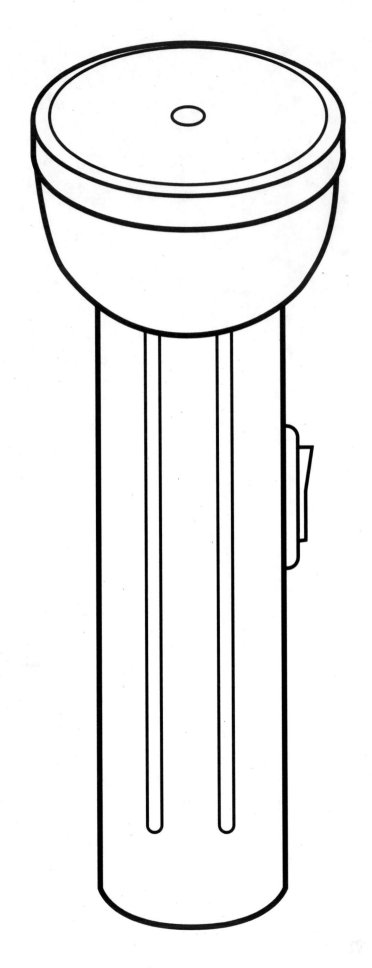

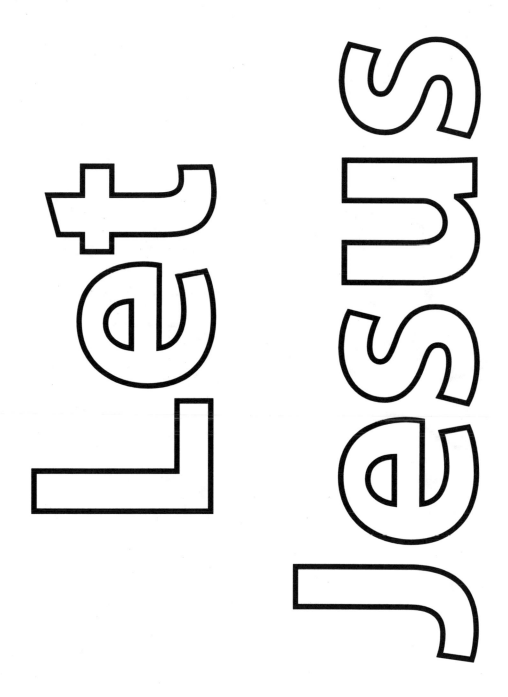

Let
Jesus

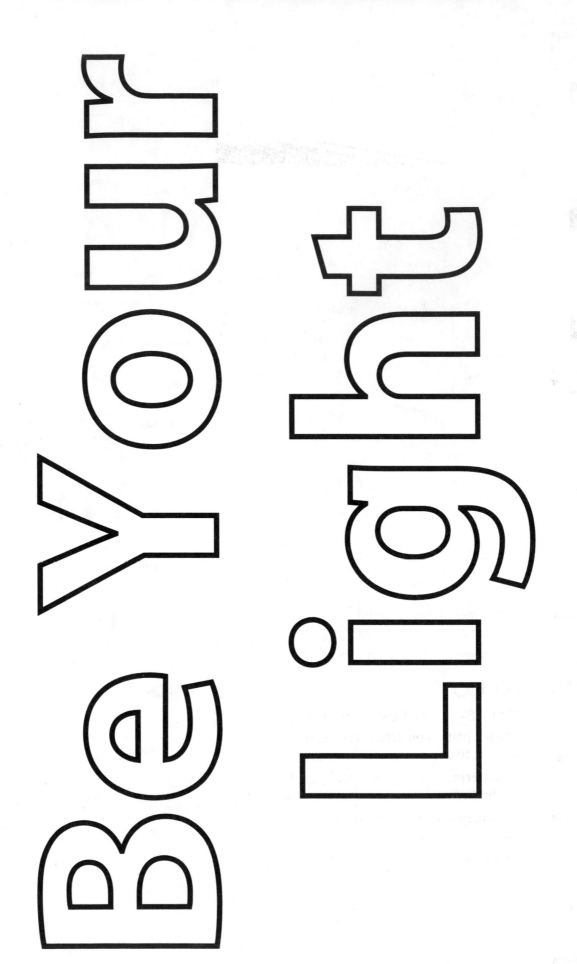

Be Your Light

Godly Men
Serve God

Suggested Usage: **Father's Day**

➤ OBJECTIVE
To promote Father's Day and godly living

➤ WHAT YOU NEED
- orange poster paper
- money pattern from pages 28-29
- green and black construction paper
- money border from page 17
- lettering from pages 30-31

➤ WHAT TO DO
1. Attach the orange poster paper to the board.
2. Copy the money pattern on green construction paper. Attach it to the center of the board.
3. Copy the lettering on black paper and attach it to the board.
4. Copy the money border, cut it out and attach it around the board's perimeter.

➤ FELLOWSHIP
This bulletin board can be used in your congregation's Father Day celebration. As a reminder of the day, copy the dollar bill from page 17 for each man in your church. Write "Godly Men Serve God" and the following

Scripture on the back of each: "No one can serve two masters. Either he will hate the one and love the other, or he will be devoted to the one and despise the other. You cannot serve both God and money. Matthew 6:24." Distribute them as the men leave your church service.

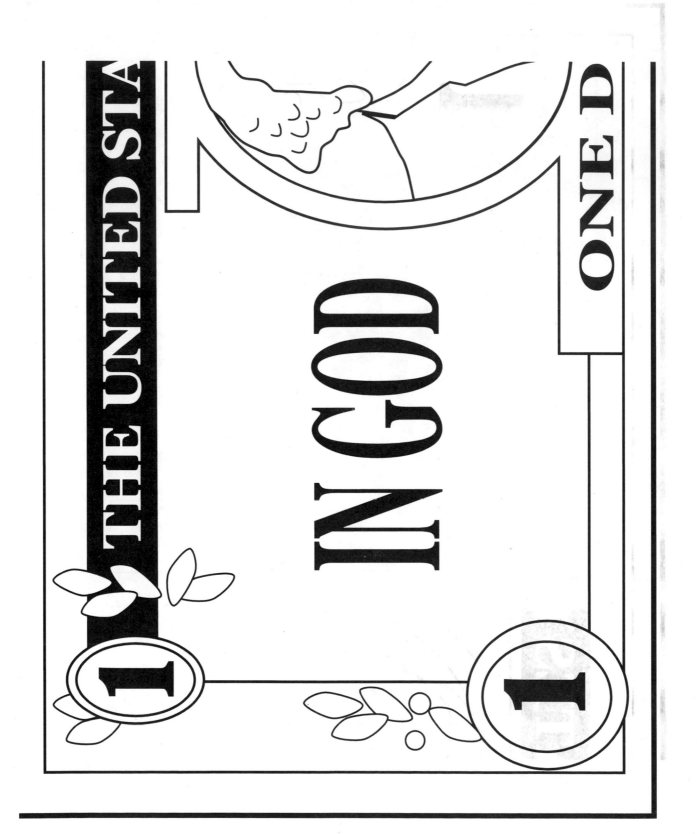

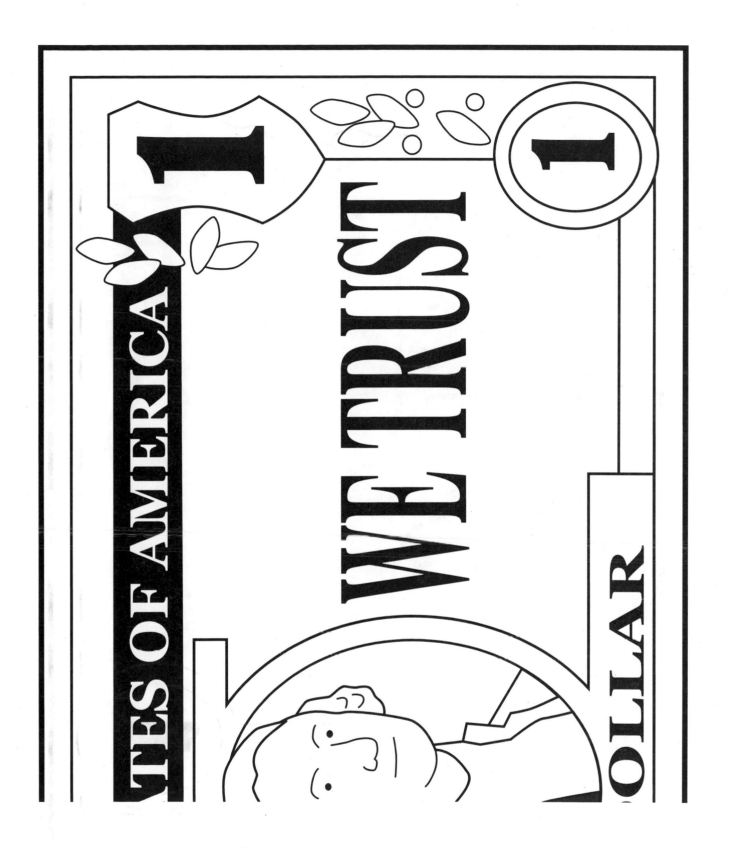

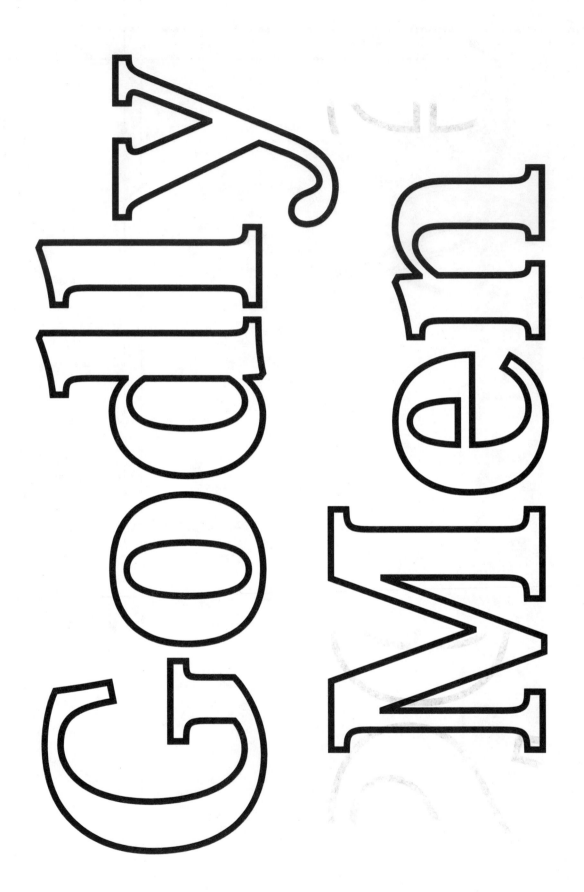

Godly Men

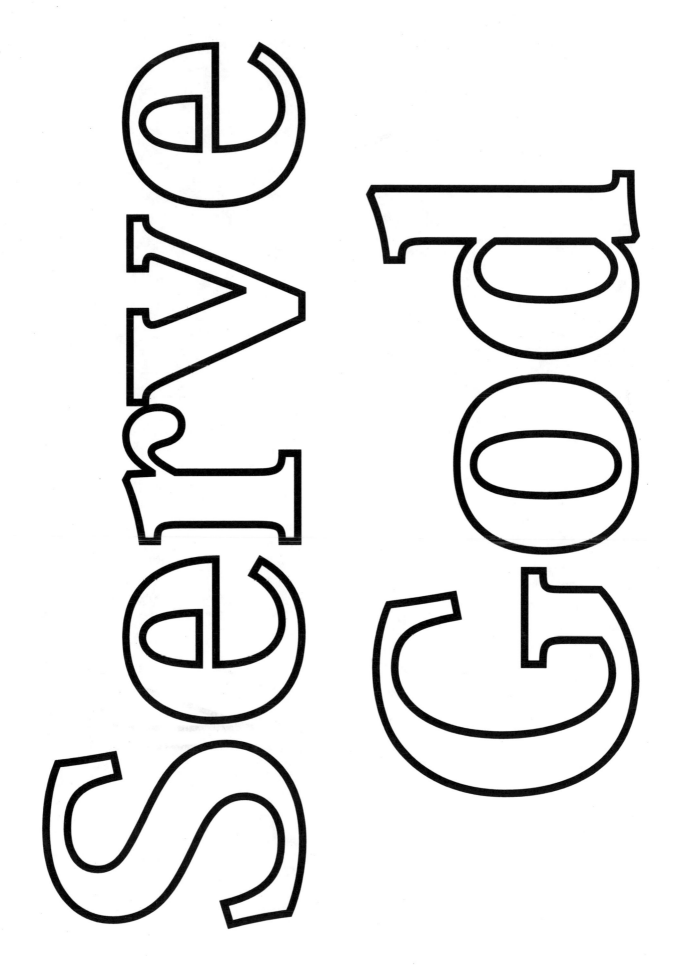

Make Some Noise
Proclaim Christ

Suggested Usage: **Independence Day**

➤ OBJECTIVE

To promote evangelism and freedom in Christ

➤ WHAT YOU NEED

- blue poster paper
- red and white construction paper
- silver glitter paint pen
- pattern for firecracker from page 33
- pattern for lettering from pages 34-35
- pattern for firecracker border from page 19

➤ WHAT TO DO

1. Attach the blue poster paper to the board.

2. Copy the firecracker pattern several times on red paper. Cut them out and attach them to the board.

3. Draw the firecrackers' fuses and lights with a silver glitter paint pen.

4. Duplicate the lettering on white paper, cut it out and attach it to the board.

5. Copy the firecracker border on red paper, cut it out and attach it around the board's perimeter.

➤ FELLOWSHIP

Arrange to attend a local fireworks show as a church group or have a show at your church. Before the fireworks display, have your pastor emphasize that only Christ can give true freedom. Sing patriotic songs! If you decide to hold your own fireworks show, consult your state's fireworks laws and have a qualified person supervise the show.

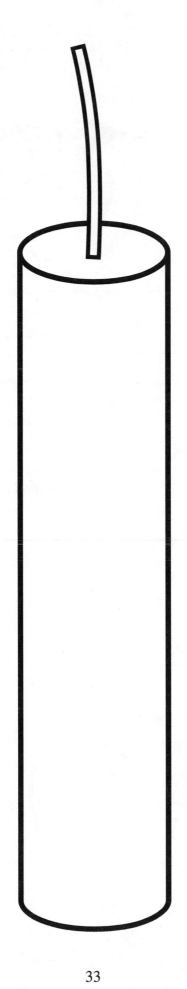

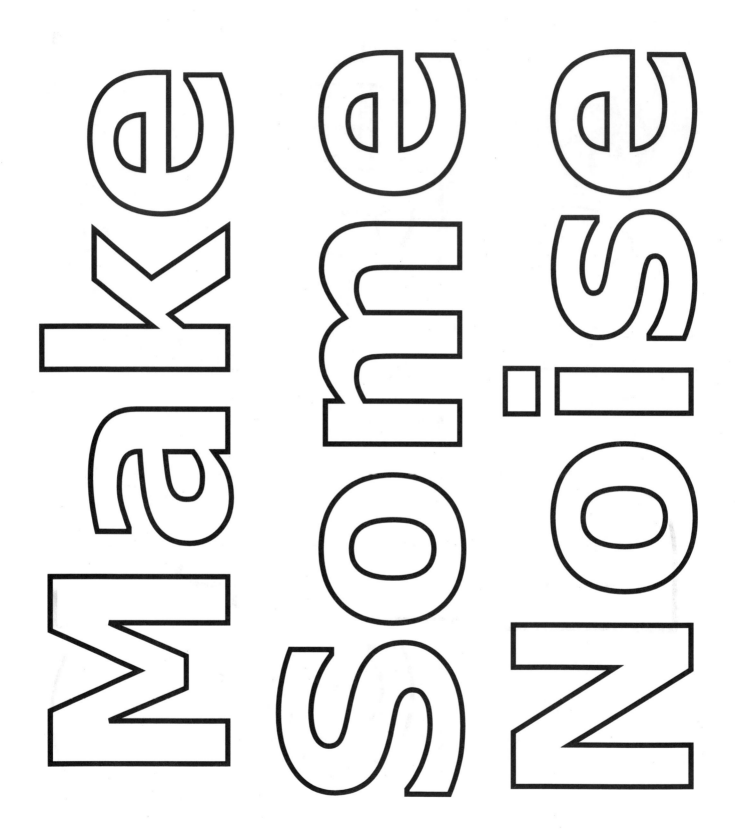

Our Symbol of Freedom

Suggested Usage: **Independence Day**

➤ OBJECTIVE

To promote symbols of Christian freedom

➤ WHAT YOU NEED

- white poster paper
- blue and red construction paper
- square pattern from page 38
- cross pattern from page 37
- lettering patterns from pages 39-40

➤ WHAT TO DO

1. Attach the white poster paper to the board.

2. Copy the square on blue paper and attach it to the upper left corner of the board.

3. Copy the cross on red paper and attach it in the center of the blue square.

4. Duplicate the lettering on red paper, cut it out and attach it in the center of the white part of the flag.

➤ FELLOWSHIP

Encourage your church's Sunday school classes to design flags on white paper that represent freedom. They can make one flag as a combined class effort or create individual ones. Mount the completed flags around the outside area of the bulletin board. Freedom's symbols are as diverse as the people drawing them!

Our Symbol

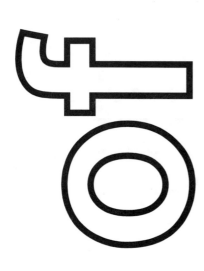

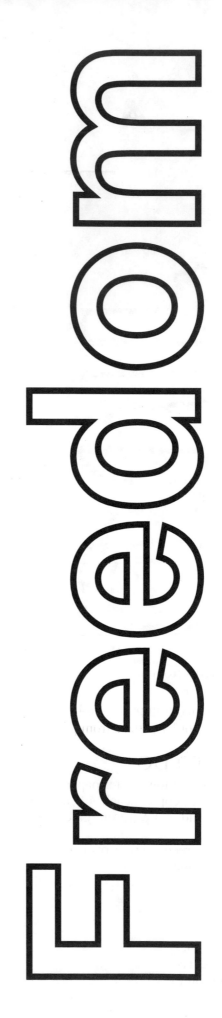

of

Freedom

A Slice of the Good Life

Suggested Usage: **General**

➤ OBJECTIVE
To promote spiritual growth

➤ WHAT YOU NEED
- yellow poster paper
- green, red, yellow and black construction paper
- white chalk or crayon
- green rind pattern from page 42
- yellow rind patterns from page 43
- red center pattern from page 44
- seed patterns from page 45
- black marker
- letter patterns from pages 46-48
- geometric border pattern from page 19

➤ WHAT TO DO
1. Attach the yellow poster paper to the board.
2. Make two copies each of the green and yellow rind patterns on green and yellow paper.
3. Flip one green section over and match it up with the other to make the watermelon rind. Tape the two together or staple them together on the board.
4. Do the same with the yellow rind, but attach it on top of the green section. Be sure to leave space on the green rind for writing.
5. Copy the red center of the watermelon and attach it on top of the yellow layer. Again, be careful to leave space for writing on the yellow layer.
6. On the green rind, use a black marker to write: Salvation — Born again experience — Jesus is Lord of your life.
7. On the yellow rind write: Sanctification — Holy Spirit indwelling — Jesus is in control of your life.
8. Copy and cut out the seeds. Use white chalk or a white crayon to write the attributes of "the good life" on the seeds, such as: joy, peace, eternal life. Attach these to the red part of the watermelon.
9. Duplicate the lettering on red paper, cut it out and attach it to the board.
10. Duplicate the geometric border on black paper, cut it out and attach it around the board's perimeter.

➤ FELLOWSHIP
Looking for a fun, refreshing and inexpensive way to spend time together as a congregation in the hot summer months? Have a "Watermelon Bash" after an evening service at your church. Remember to chill the watermelons ahead of time. Include a Watermelon Eating Contest in your event. Create separate "heats" for each age level. Award the winners a packet of watermelon seeds.

41

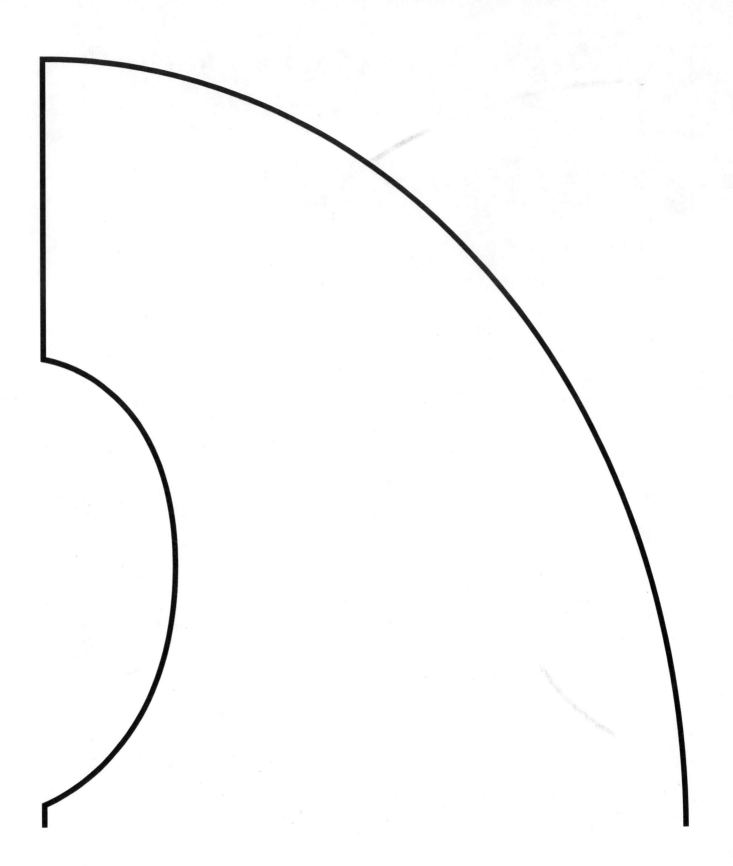

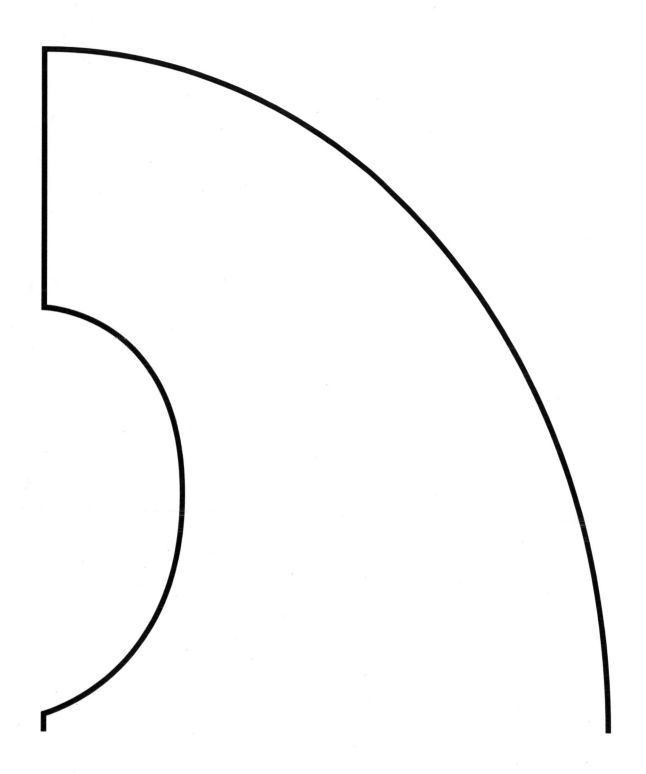

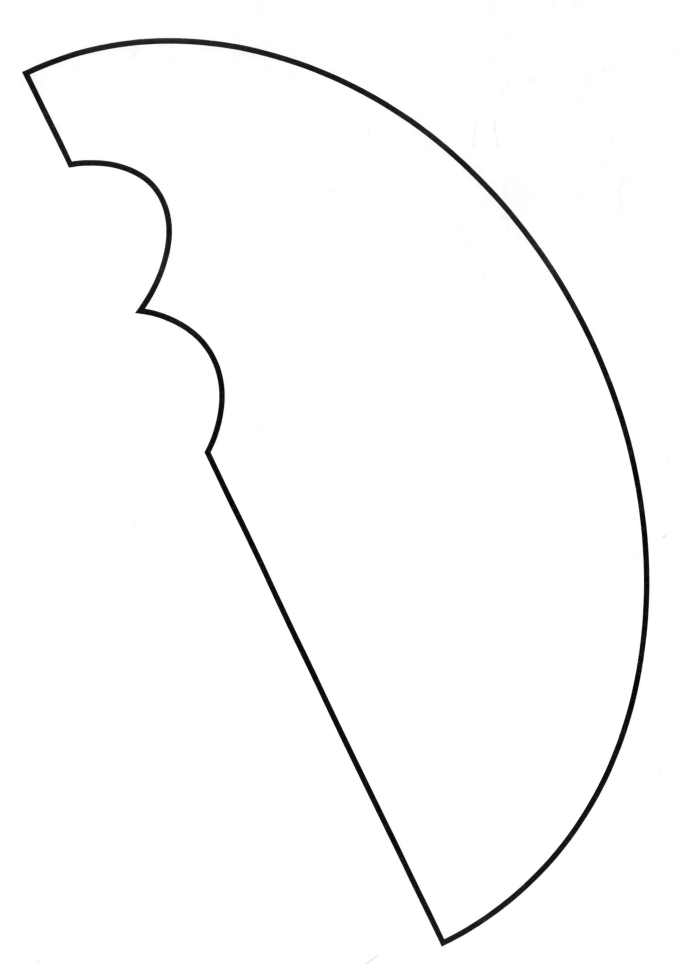

44

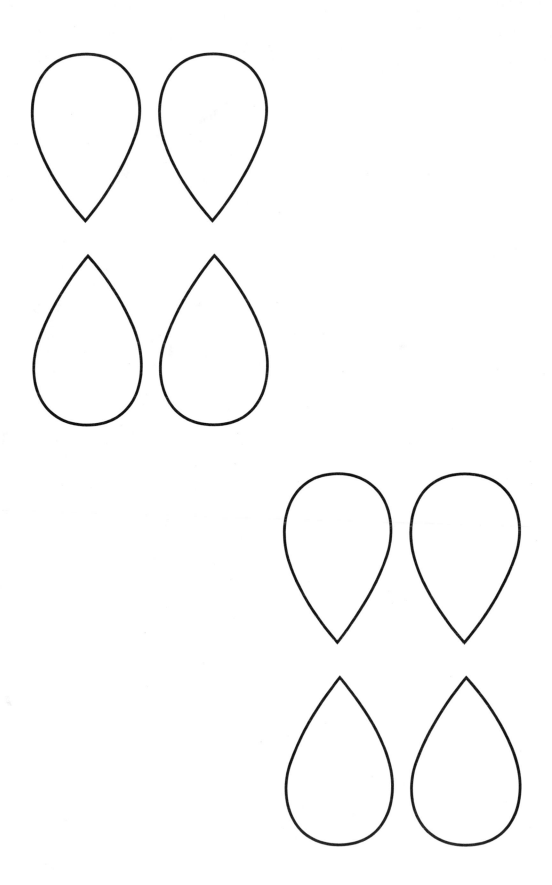

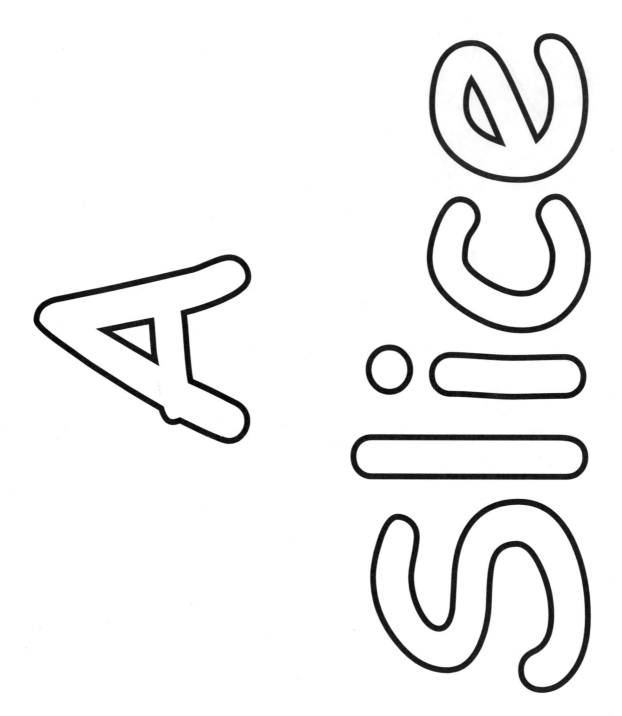

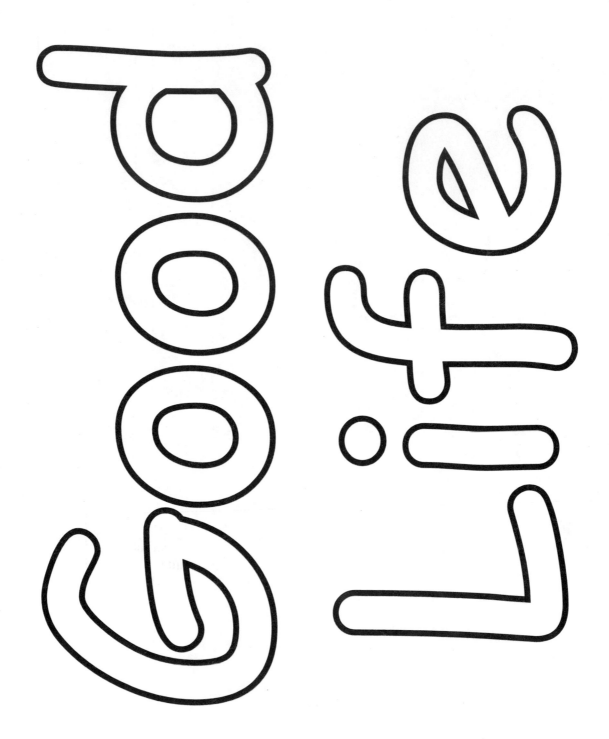

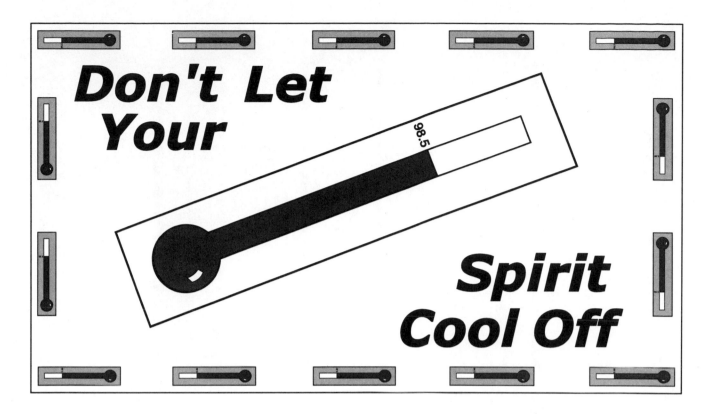

Suggested Usage: **General**

➤ OBJECTIVE

To promote spiritual growth and enthusiasm

➤ WHAT YOU NEED

- yellow poster paper
- white and red construction paper
- red marker
- thermometer patterns from pages 50-51
- lettering patterns from pages 52-54
- thermometer border from page 21

➤ WHAT TO DO

1. Attach the yellow poster paper to the board.

2. Copy the thermometer patterns and tape them together on back.

3. On the thermometer, color the mercury reader red up to 98.5.

4. Attach the thermometer to the board.

5. Duplicate the lettering on red paper, cut it out and attach it to the board as shown.

6. Duplicate the thermometer border, cut it out and attach it around the board's perimeter.

➤ FELLOWSHIP

Is your church growing "cool" in spirit? Increase your congregation's enthusiasm for God with a spiritual enrichment day conference at your church (one fun title you could use: "Get Hot for God"). Give your pastor a rest and enlist outside guest speakers who have a track record in Christian motivational speaking. Consider a catered or pot luck lunch so attendees can relax together and discuss what they are learning. Recruit several teens to babysit younger children during the conference.

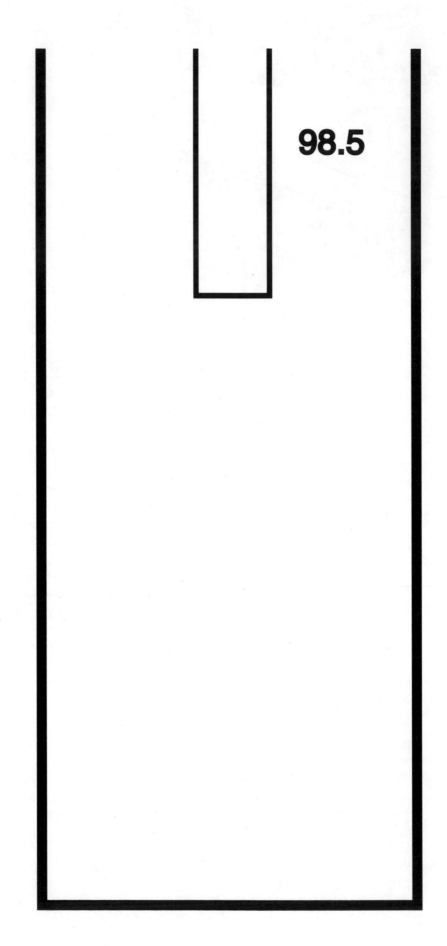

98.5

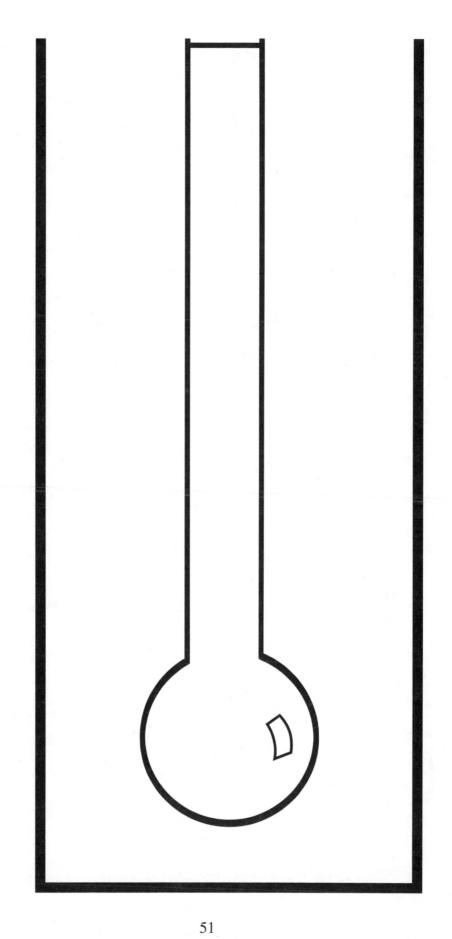

Don't Let

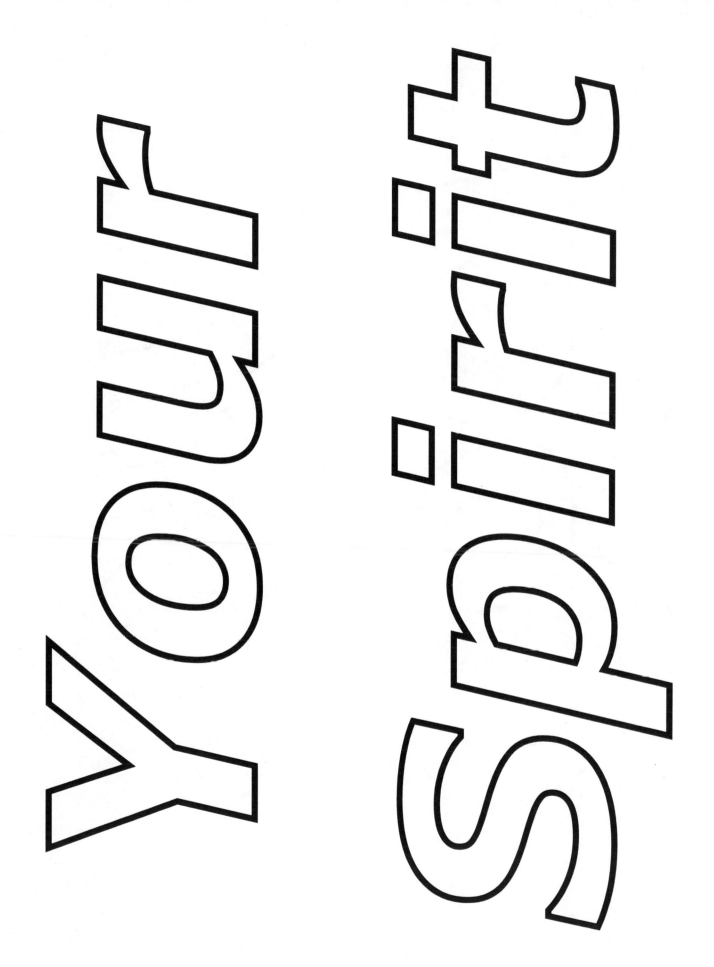

Cool off

Dig Into Prayer

Suggested Usage: **General**

➤ OBJECTIVE
To promote spiritual growth and prayer

➤ WHAT YOU NEED
- brown poster paper
- bucket pattern from page 56
- shovel pattern from page 57
- starfish pattern from page 58
- blue, red, yellow and orange construction paper
- purple marker
- black yarn
- shell border from page 19
- lettering from pages 59-60

➤ WHAT TO DO
1. Attach the brown poster paper to the board.
2. Copy the bucket pattern on blue paper. Write "Let Jesus" on the bucket with a purple marker. Attach the bucket to the board.
3. Attach a yarn handle to the bucket.
4. Copy the shovel pattern on red paper. Write "mold" on the handle with the purple marker. Attach it to the board.
5. Copy the starfish pattern on yellow paper. Write "you" on it with a purple marker. Attach it to the board.
6. Copy the lettering on orange paper, cut it out and attach it to the board.
7. Copy the shell border, cut it out and attach it around the board's perimeter.

➤ FELLOWSHIP
Encourage the congregation to commit to pray at least 15 minutes each day for the entire month. Have them use "The Lord's Prayer" in Matthew 6:9-13 as an example. Explain that they should use this prayer as an example, focusing on the phrases and adding in their own prayers rather than simply reciting the written prayer.

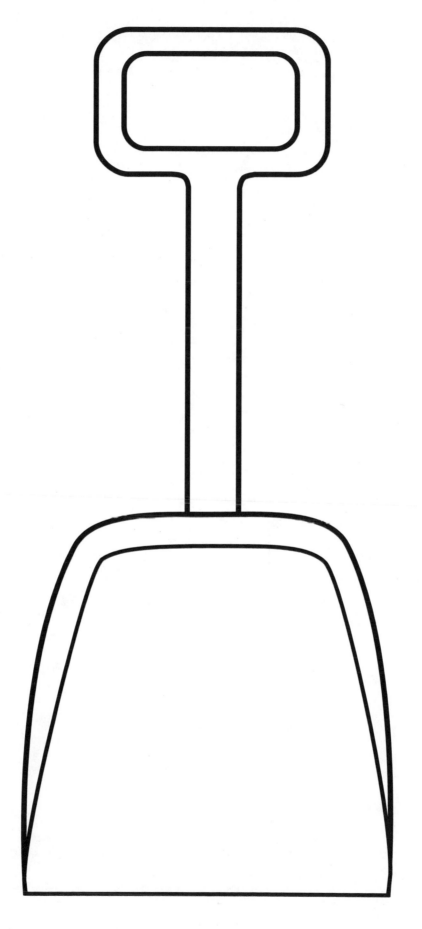

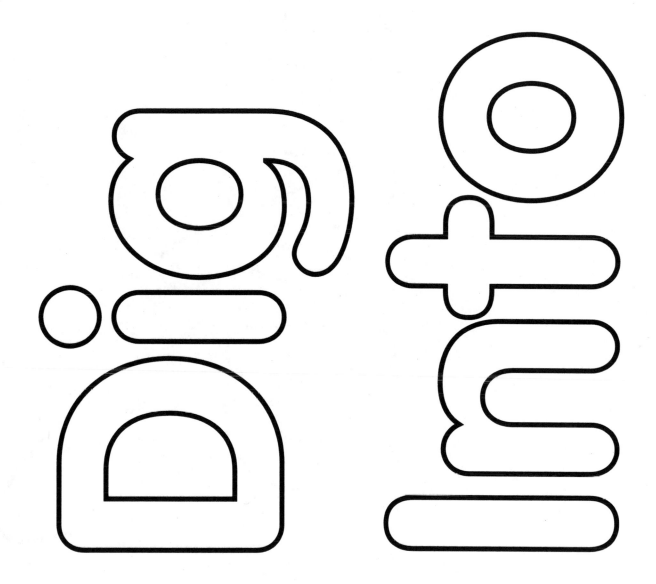

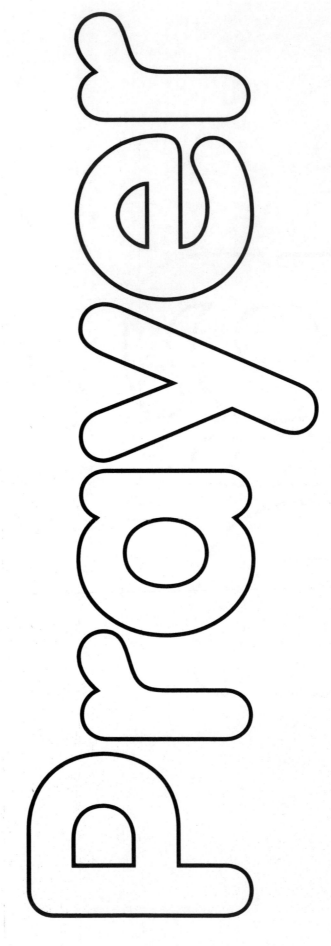

Suggested Usage: **General**

➤ OBJECTIVE

To promote Bible study

➤ WHAT YOU NEED

- red poster paper
- gas gauge patterns from pages 62-63
- Bible patterns from pages 64-65
- assorted colors of construction paper
- colored markers
- lettering from pages 66-67
- car border from page 17

➤ WHAT TO DO

1. Attach the red poster paper to the board.

2. Copy the gas gauge patterns on white paper, tape them together in back and attach the whole gas gauge to the board.

3. Draw a red line to "E" on the gas gauge with a marker.

4. Copy the Bible pages pattern on white paper. Copy the Bible cover pattern on black paper. Ttape them together in back and attach the whole open Bible to the board.

5. Write "Read Daily" in the open Bible.

6. Copy the lettering on black paper, cut it out and attach it to the board.

7. Copy the car border on various colors of paper, cut it out and attach it around the board's perimeter.

➤ FELLOWSHIP

Ask your congregation to individually commit to reading one Bible chapter each day for the entire month (Proverbs — which has 31 chapters — is a good month-long read). Explain this program during church announcements and have it printed in your worship bulletin (homebound parishioners will also enjoy participating). Ask those who commit to the reading plan to write their names on one of the cars along the bulletin board border.

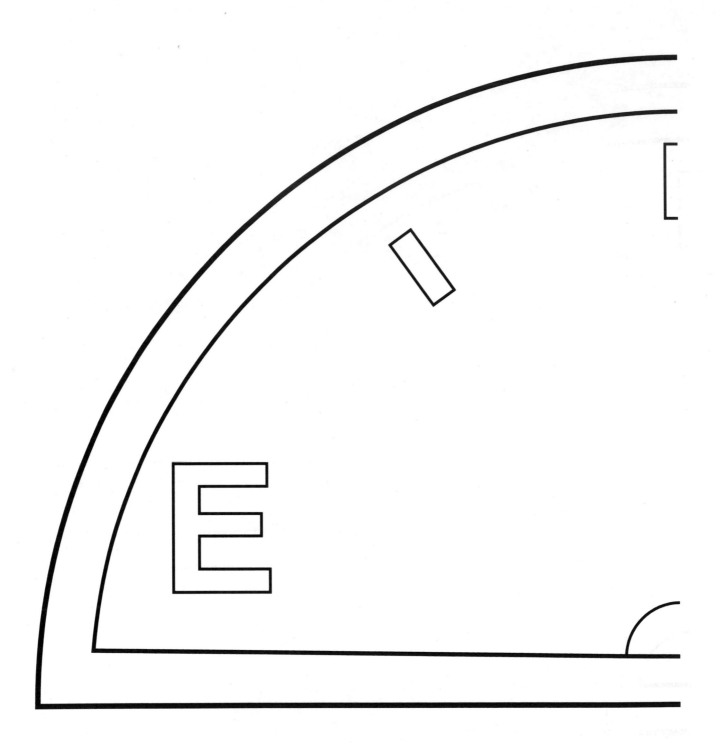

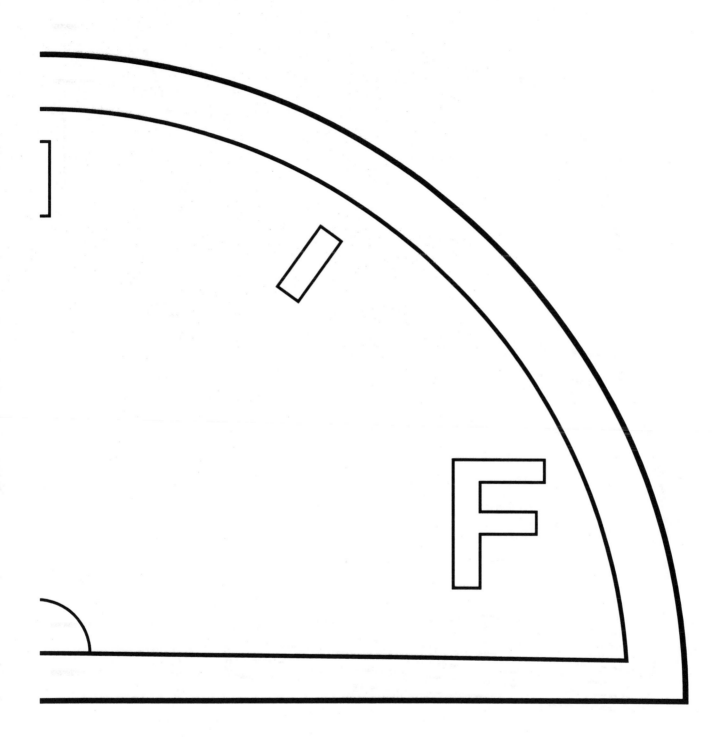

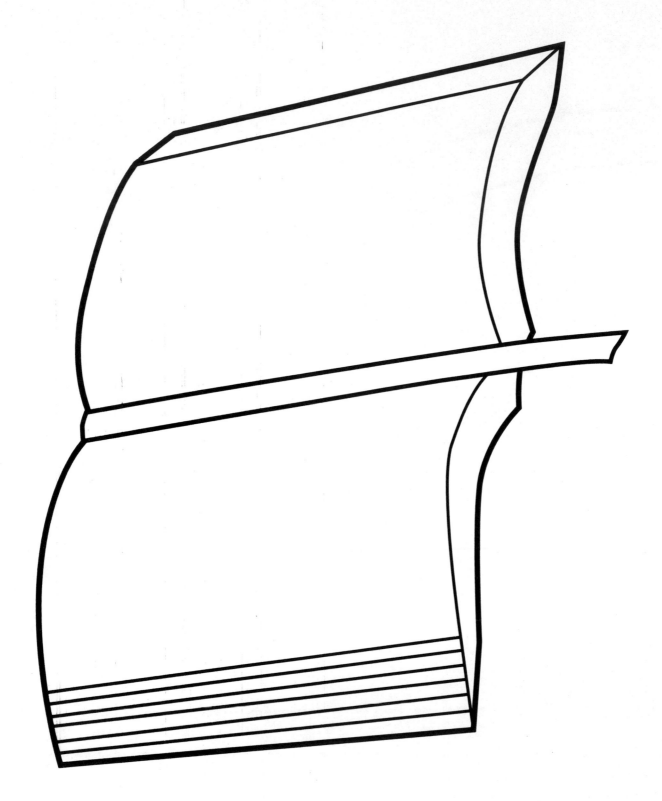

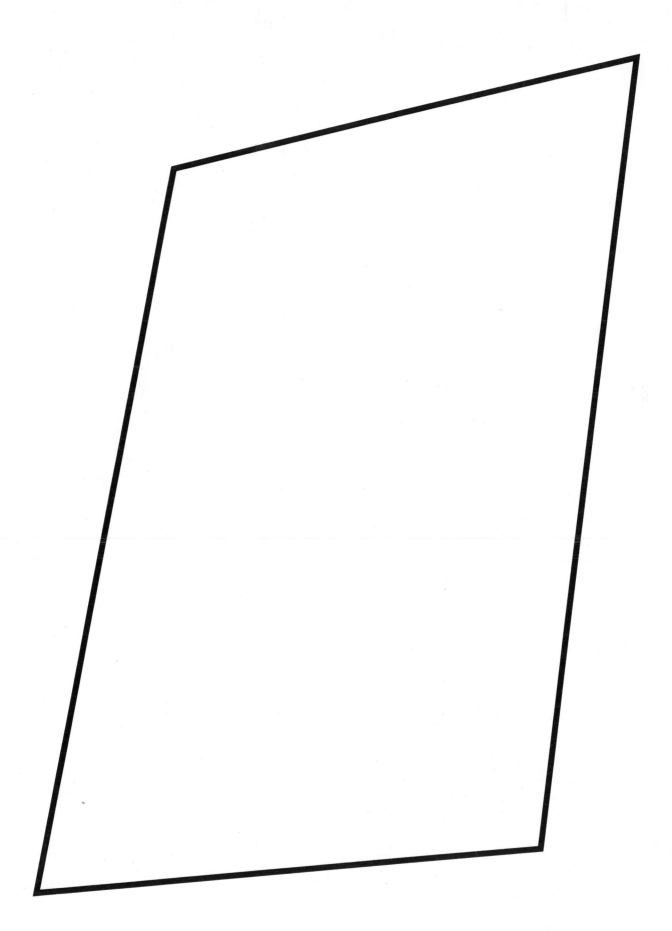

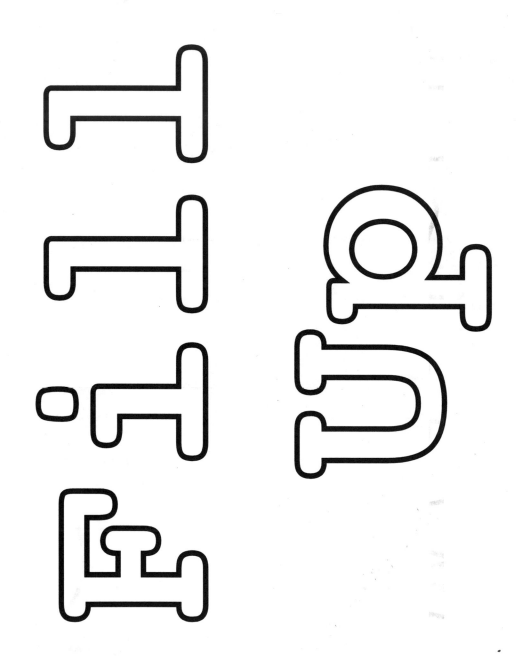

with the Gospel

Suggested Usage: **General**

➤ OBJECTIVE
To promote faithfulness and encouragement

➤ WHAT YOU NEED
- blue poster paper
- colored paper
- clothespin pattern from page 73
- shirt patterns on pages 69-70
- pants patterns on pages 71-72
- fabric
- yarn or twine
- black marker
- clothespin border from page 17
- lettering patterns from page 74
- clothing notes on page 75

➤ WHAT TO DO
1. Attach the blue poster paper to the board.
2. Attach yarn or twine across the board to look like a clothesline.
3. Copy the clothespins on brown construction paper. Write "Jesus," "Pray," "Study" and "Read" on the clothespins with a black marker.
4. Copy the shirt and pants patterns. Tape the shirt patterns together on the back. Do the same with the pants patterns.
5. Glue fabric on the shirt and pants as desired to add interest.
6. Attach the shirt and pants to the clothesline. Attach two clothespins at the top of each.
7. Copy the lettering on black paper, cut it out and attach it below the clothes.
8. Copy the clothespin border on brown paper, cut it out and attach it around the board's perimeter.

➤ FELLOWSHIP
Copy the clothing notes from page 75 on colored paper. Glue a yarn "clothesline" to each. Distribute the notes to members of your congregation who want to send a word of encouragement to friends who are struggling. Suggest that they follow up the note with a phone call or invitation for coffee or lunch to add a personal touch.

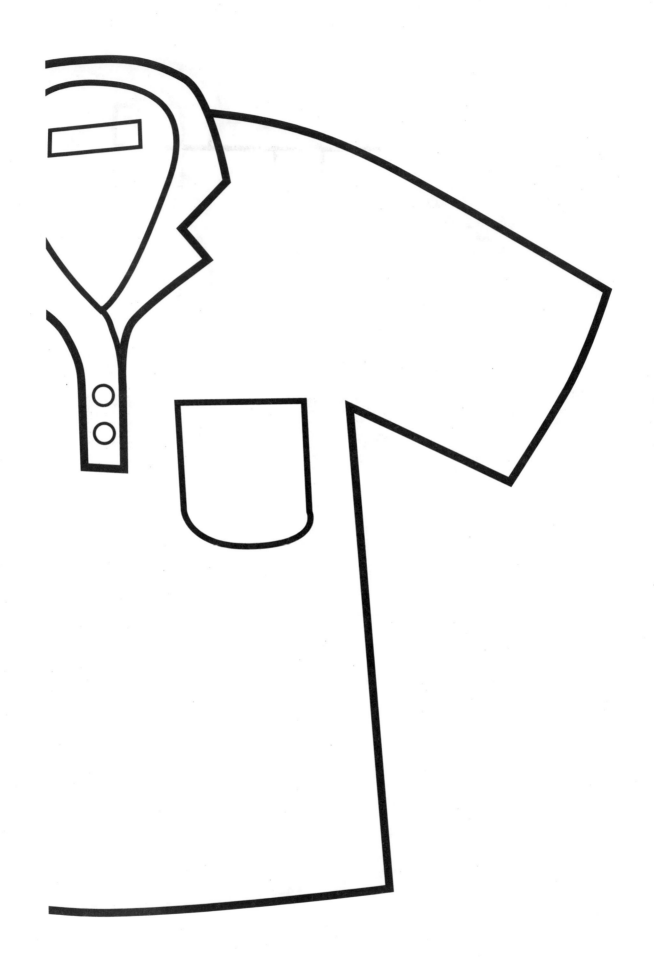

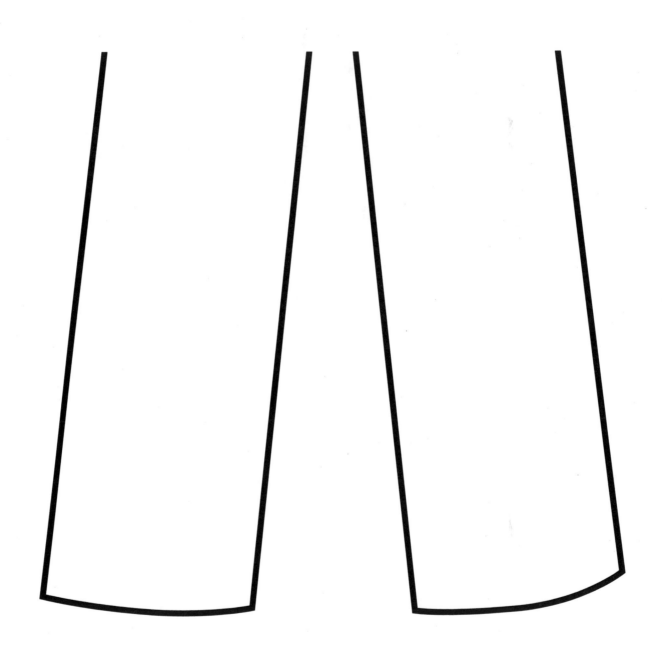

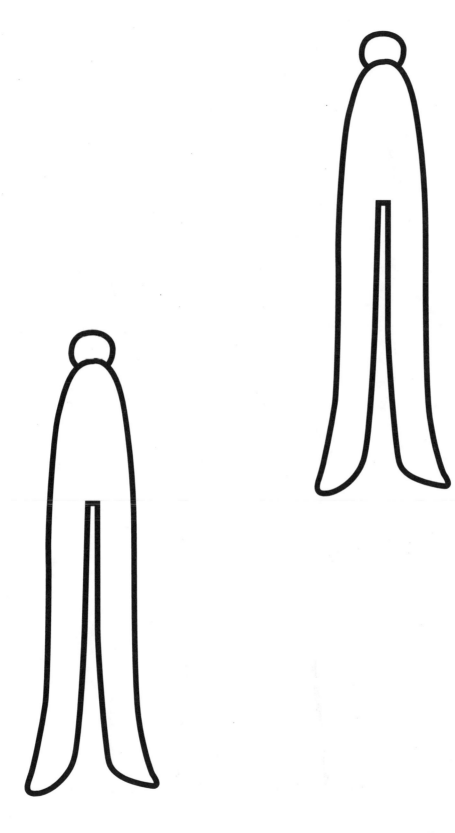

HANG IN THERE

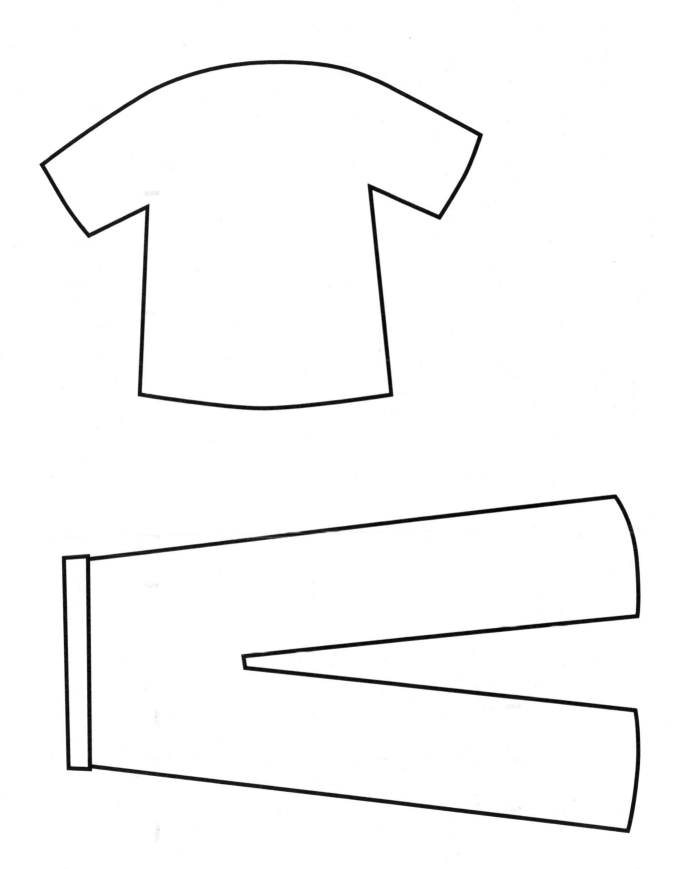

Suggested Usage: **General**

➤ OBJECTIVE

To evangelize and promote Jesus

➤ WHAT YOU NEED

- blue, brown and orange poster paper
- orange yarn
- green and black construction paper
- cacti patterns on pages 77-80
- brown marker
- patterns for lettering on pages 81-82
- pattern for thermometer border on page 21
- handout on page 83

➤ WHAT TO DO

1. Attach blue poster paper to the board for the sky, covering about 3/4 of the board from the top.

2. Cut a rounded shape from orange paper and attach it to the center of the blue paper.

3. Create rays for the sun by attaching lengths of orange yarn.

4. Attach brown poster paper for the desert floor. Make distant hills if desired.

5. Copy the three cacti on green paper using the pattern. Attach them to the board.

6. Draw a tumbleweed on the board with a brown marker.

7. Copy the lettering on black paper and attach it across the top of the board.

8. Copy the thermometer border, cut it out and attach it around the board's perimeter.

➤ FELLOWSHIP

Register to staff a booth advertising your church at your local county fair or a community event. Distribute fliers with your church's service times, special programs for youth or children, nursery facilities, etc. Also, give a free cup of water to each person, in the name of Jesus. Include the handout on page 83 to draw people closer to God and explain the biblical significance of the cup of water. This is a wonderful community service ministry that will let people get to know your church!

We hope this water refreshes you. Read on to see what happened one time when Jesus stopped for a cool drink of water.

Jesus came to a town in Samaria called Sychar, near the plot of ground Jacob had given to his son Joseph. Jacob's well was there, and Jesus, tired as he was from the journey, sat down by the well. It was about the sixth hour.

When a Samaritan woman came to draw water, Jesus said to her, "Will you give me a drink?" (His disciples had gone into the town to buy food.)

The Samaritan woman said to Him, "You are a Jew and I am a Samaritan woman. How can you ask me for a drink?" (For Jews [did] not associate with Samaritans.)

Jesus answered her, "If you knew the gift of God and who it is that asks you for a drink, you would have asked him and he would have given you living water."

"Sir," the woman said, "You have nothing to draw with and the well is deep. Where can you get this living water? Are you greater than our father Jacob, who gave us the well and drank from it himself, as did also his sons and his flocks and herds?"

Jesus answered, "Everyone who drinks this water will be thirsty again, but whoever drinks the water I give him will never thirst. Indeed, the water I give him will become in him a spring of water welling up to eternal life."

The woman said to him, "Sir, give me this water so that I won't get thirsty and have to keep coming here to draw water." He told her, "Go, call your husband and come back."

"I have no husband," she replied.

Jesus said to her, "You are right when you say you have no husband. The fact is, you have had five husbands, and the man you now have is not your husband. What you have just said is quite true."

"Sir," the woman said, "I can see that you are a prophet. Our fathers worshiped on this mountain, but you Jews claim that the place where we must worship is in Jerusalem."

Jesus declared, "Believe me, woman, a time is coming when you will worship the Father neither on this mountain nor in Jerusalem. You Samaritans worship what you do not know; we worship what we do know, for salvation is from the Jews. Yet a time is coming and has now come when the true worshipers will worship the Father in spirit and truth, for they are the kind of worshipers the Father seeks. God is spirit, and His worshipers must worship in spirit and in truth."

The woman said, "I know that Messiah" (called Christ) "is coming. When he comes, he will explain everything to us."

Then Jesus declared, "I who speak to you am He."

Just then His disciples returned and were surprised to find him talking with a woman. But no one asked, "What do you want?" or "Why are you talking with her?"

Then, leaving her water jar, the woman went back to the town and said to the people, "Come, see a man who told me everything I ever did. Could this be the Christ?" They came out of the town and made their way toward Him.

— John 4:5-30

Suggested Usage: **General**

➤ OBJECTIVE

To promote God's guidance and peace

➤ WHAT YOU NEED

- blue poster paper
- balloon patterns from pages 85-87
- black marker
- assorted colors of construction paper
- yarn
- glue
- lettering patterns from page 88-89
- cloud border from page 17

➤ WHAT TO DO

1. Attach the blue poster paper to the board.
2. Copy the two balloon sections on colored paper or copy them on white and color them.
3. Copy the basket on brown paper.
4. Glue lengths of yarn from the basket to the balloon.

5. Enlarge three copies of the cloud border pattern on gray paper.
6. Use a black marker to write one word on each cloud: "problems," "doubts" or "worries." Attach the clouds to the board.
7. Duplicate the lettering on yellow paper, cut it out and attach it to the board.
8. Copy the cloud border on white paper, cut them out and attach them around the board's perimeter.

➤ FELLOWSHIP

Organize a group from your congregation to volunteer at a local soup kitchen for a couple of weeks. Focusing on other's problems is a good way to "Rise Above It All" and realize that you are not the only one with difficulties. Volunteering will help your parishioners gain perspective on their needs and the needs in your community. Plus, you will be living out Matthew 25:35!

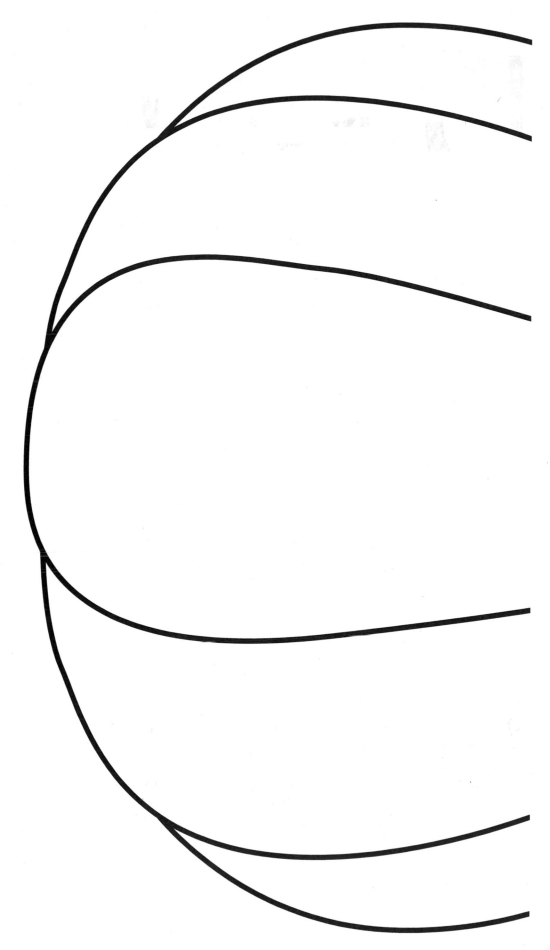

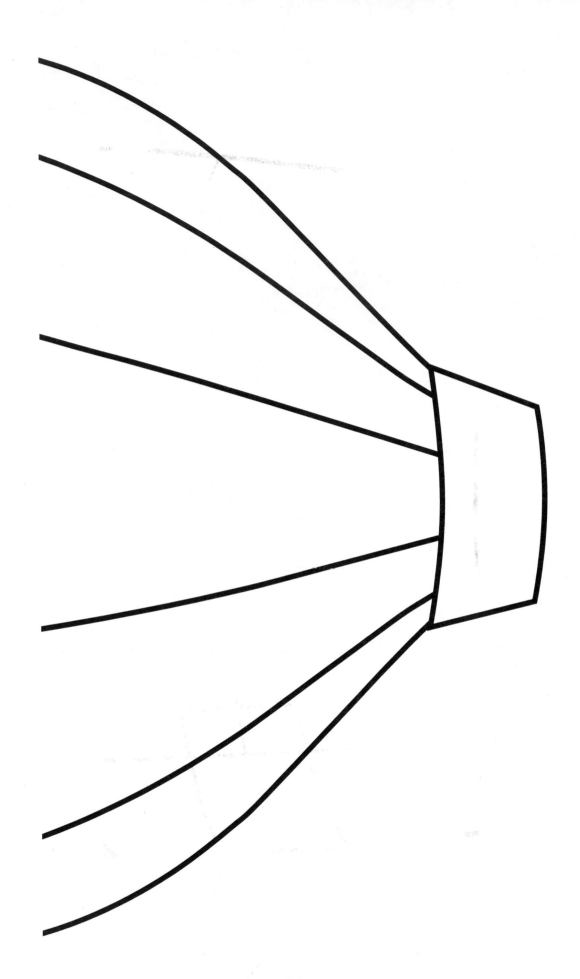

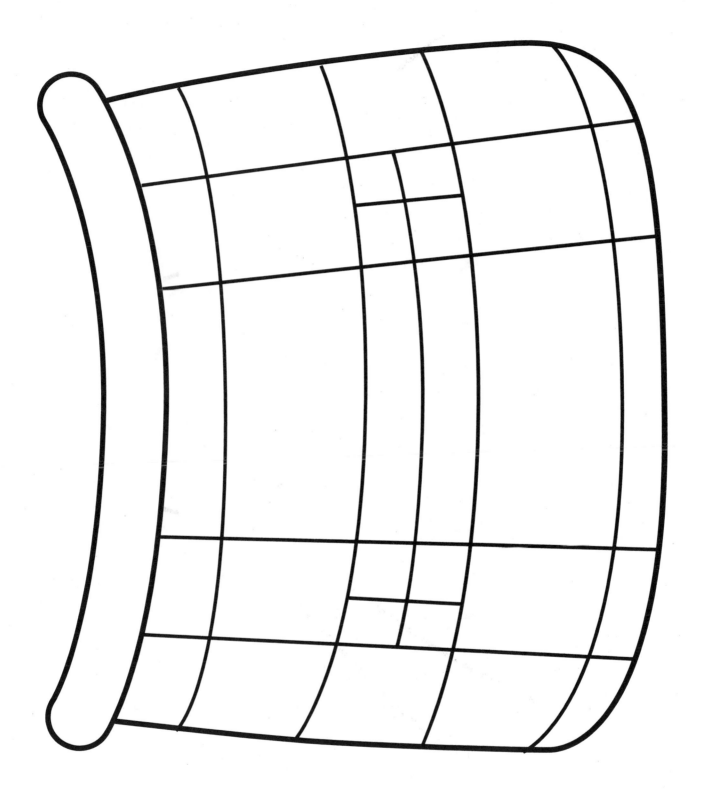

RISE

ABOVE

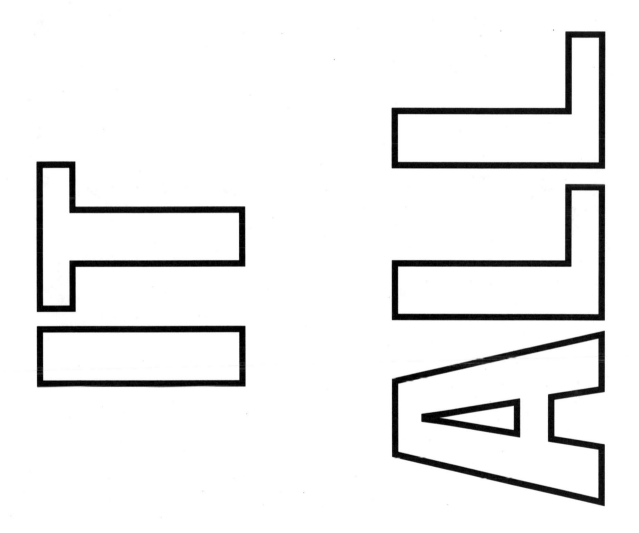

Suggested Usage: **General or Walk-a-thon**

➤ OBJECTIVE
To promote positive persistence

➤ WHAT YOU NEED
- yellow poster paper
- shoe pattern from page 91
- wing pattern from page 92
- assorted colors of construction paper
- lettering patterns form page 93-94
- shoe border from page 21
- sponsor sheet from page 95

➤ WHAT TO DO
1. Attach the yellow poster paper to the board.
2. Copy two or three of the shoe pattern on colored paper or copy it on white paper and color them in. Attach the shoes to the board.
3. Copy the wing on white paper, two for each shoe. Attach the wings to the backs of the shoes.
4. Bend the wings slightly away from the board to give a three-dimensional effect.
5. Copy the lettering on blue paper, cut it out and attach it to the board.
6. Copy the shoe border, cut it out and attach it around the board's perimeter.

➤ FELLOWSHIP
This bulletin board can be used to announce a walk-a-thon at your church. A walk-a-thon is a sponsored walk that can raise money for your church's building fund, general fund, missions or a local charity. Simply copy the sponsor sheet on page 95 for each participant. Decide the length for the walk (typically 3K, 5K or 7K) and the route. The day of the walk, open with prayer and a starting pistol. Award fun prizes for early and late finishers. Be sure to recruit volunteers to distribute water and snacks along the route!

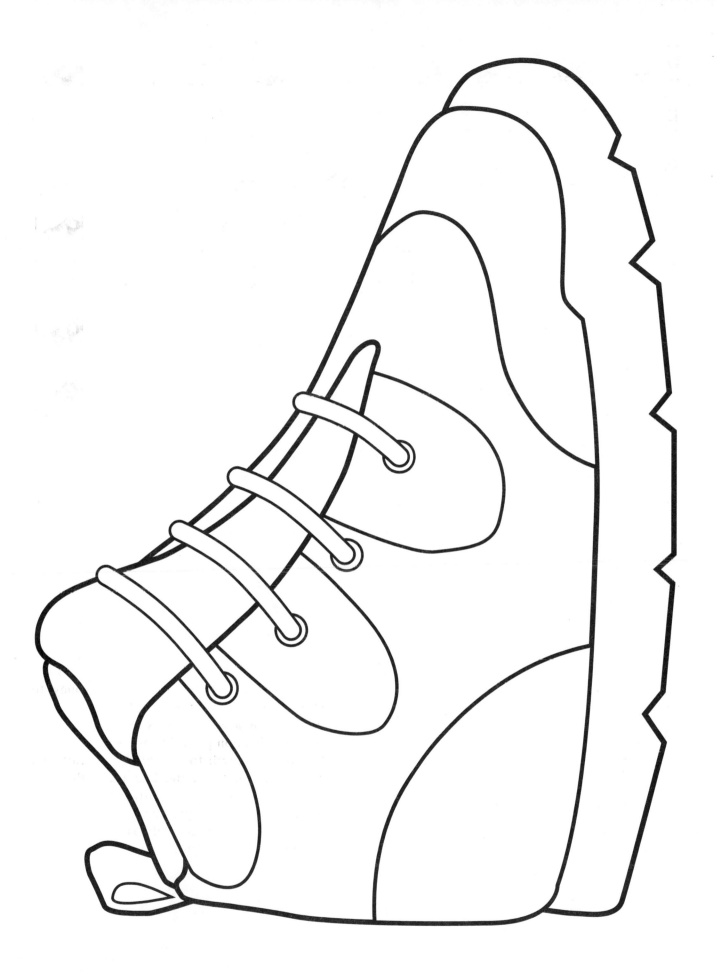

FEET RUN

Walk-a-Thon

_____ is sponsoring a walk-a-thon on _____. We are raising funds for _____. We would appreciate your support! Please indicate below the amount you wish to sponsor.

Name	Phone	$ per mile	Paid?

Suggested Usage: **General**

➤ OBJECTIVE

To promote what delights God

➤ WHAT YOU NEED

- black poster paper
- yellow, white and light blue construction paper
- pattern for moon from page 98
- pattern for star from page 99
- black marker
- lettering patterns from pages 100-101
- polyfil

➤ WHAT TO DO

1. Attach the black poster paper to the board.

2. Copy the moon pattern on yellow paper and attach it to the board.

3. Copy several stars on white paper and attach them to the board.

4. Write things that delight God on the stars with a black marker. Some suggestions: servanthood, justice, mercy, faithfulness, worship, purity and repentance.

5. Copy the lettering on light blue paper and attach it around the board's perimeter.

6. Attach polyfil around the edge of the board as a border.

➤ FELLOWSHIP

Plan to visit a planetarium as a church family outing. Or, arrange to have telescopes loaned to the church for star gazing. Taking time to focus on the solar system will help your congregation realize how great the God of the universe is. The stars are His handiwork! Summer's clear nights are the best time to enjoy these stars and think about the delights of God.

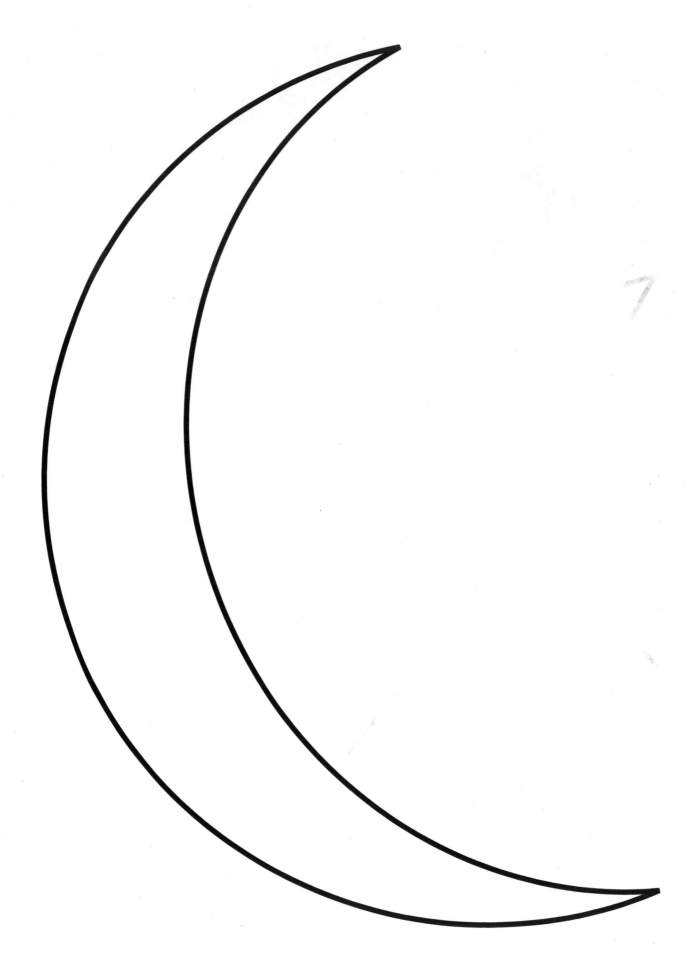

Summer Nights

and

God's

Delights

Suggested Usage: **General**

➤ **OBJECTIVE**
To promote servanthood

➤ **WHAT YOU NEED**
- green poster paper
- volleyball pattern from page 104
- black marker
- white and black construction paper
- gray nylon netting (1/2 yard)
- lettering patterns from page 105
- volleyball border pattern from page 21

➤ **WHAT TO DO**
1. Attach the green poster paper to the board.
2. Create a volleyball net from the nylon netting by cutting it to the size you need. Attach it at an angle across the board.
3. Roll black construction paper or poster paper and attach one to either end of the net as poles.
4. Copy the volleyball pattern on white paper and attach it to the board as if it were being tossed.

5. Write "Jesus" on the ball with a black marker.
6. Write "You" on the side of the net where you attached the ball.
7. Write "world" on the opposite side.
8. Copy the lettering on white paper, cut it out and attach it to the board as shown.
9. Copy the volleyball border on white paper, cut it out and attach it around the board's perimeter.

➤ **FELLOWSHIP**
On each volleyball you use for the border, write opportunities for the congregation to serve the local community by volunteering. Examples: soup kitchens, youth organizations, local missions, nursing homes, tutoring, etc. Ask others to help you with ideas for places to volunteer.

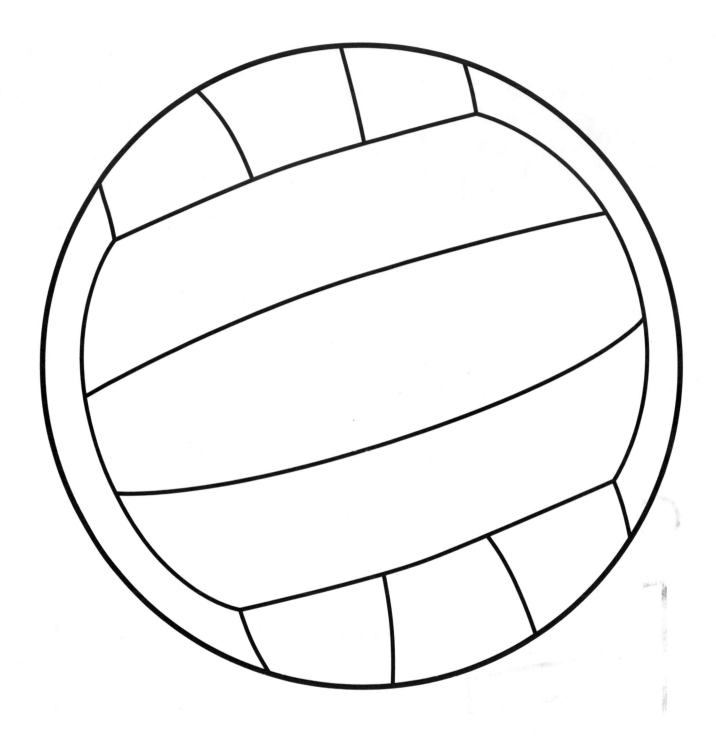

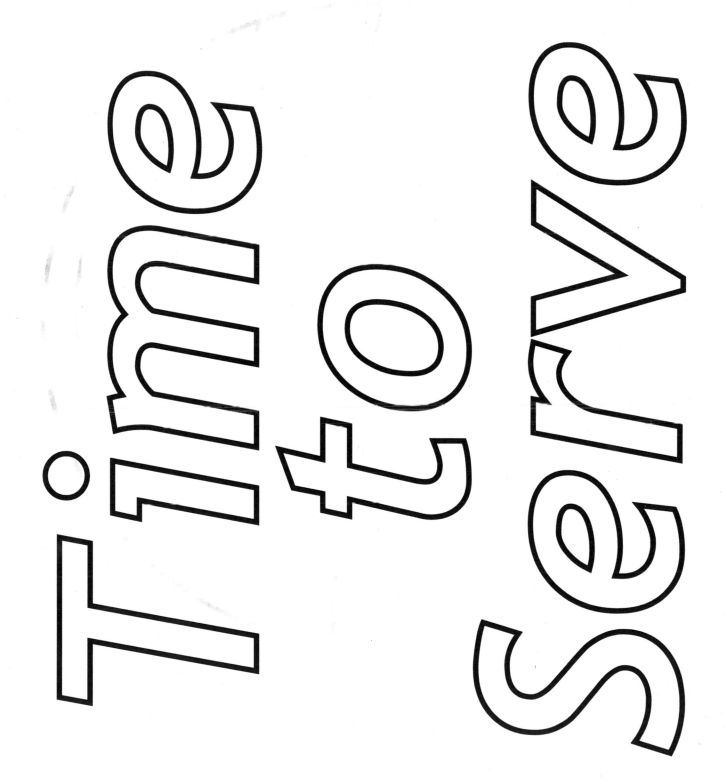

Time to
Serve

Suggested Usage: **General**

➤ OBJECTIVE
To promote Bible study

➤ WHAT YOU NEED
- red poster paper
- ice cream cone pattern from page 108
- ice cream scoop pattern from page 107
- assorted colors of construction paper
- colored markers
- lettering patterns from pages 109-110
- ice cream cone border from page 19
- handout on page 111

➤ WHAT TO DO
1. Attach the red poster paper to the board.
2. Copy the ice cream cone on brown paper. Attach it to the board.
3. Copy the ice cream scoop on two different colors of construction paper.
4. Write "Old Testament" on one scoop and "New Testament" on the other. Attach these to the top of the cone.
5. Copy the lettering onto assorted colors of paper, cut it out and attach it to the board.
6. Copy the ice cream cone border on white paper, color the ice cream varying colors and attach these to the board's perimeter.

➤ FELLOWSHIP
Copy the handout on page 111 and place a stack near the board to encourage Bible study and reading for the month.

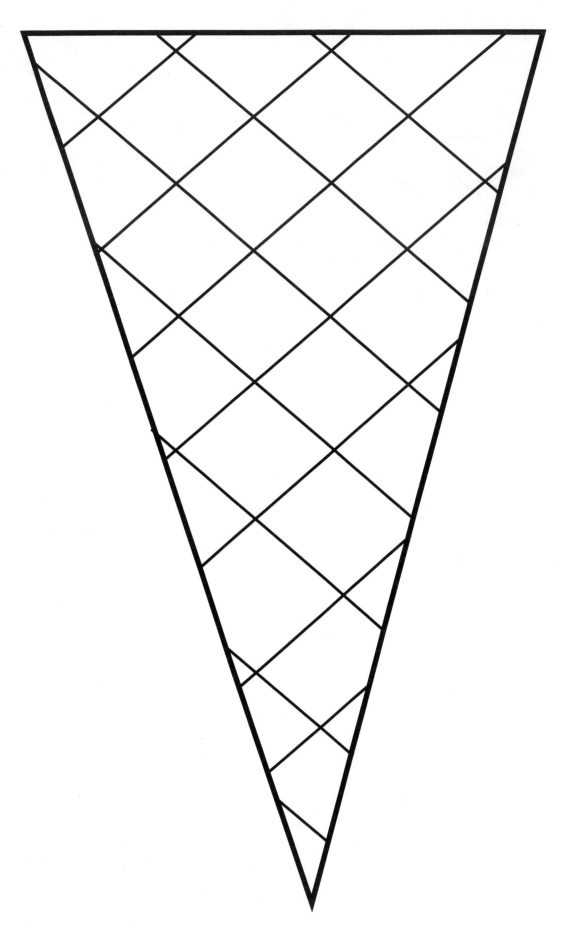

Try All 66 Flavors

in God's Word

Books of the Bible

Old Testament

Genesis: The book of origins.

Exodus: Means "departure" or "going out."

Leviticus: God's plan for His people to approach Him.

Numbers: Laws, regulations and experiences of the Israelites in the wilderness.

Deuteronomy: Renewal of the covenant.

Joshua: Continues the history of Israel.

Judges: Leaders who delivered Israel.

Ruth: Moabitess who became a worshiper of God.

1 and 2 Samuel: God rules in the lives of men and nations.

1 and 2 Kings: Named for their contents.

1 and 2 Chronicles: Preserves proper priesthood and worship.

Ezra: Fulfillment of God's promise.

Nehemiah: Rebuilding the walls of Jerusalem and fidelity to the Law.

Esther: Divine judgment.

Job: Problems with suffering and evil.

Psalm: Songs from the heart.

Proverbs: Teaching by contrasts.

Ecclesiastes: Fleeting pleasures lead to disaster.

Song of Songs: A poem of love.

Isaiah: Prophet who protested the unfaithfulness of Israel.

Jeremiah: Prophet who spoke of judgment.

Lamentations: Songs of mourning.

Ezekiel: The fall and restoration of Israel.

Daniel: Cultural and religious changes are forced.

Hosea: Unfaithfulness of Israel.

Joel: Locusts and drought devastation.

Amos: Reveals spiritual corruption in religious formalism.

Obadiah: Sense of justice.

Jonah: God wants to deal with man in mercy.

Micah: Greed in the hearts of leaders.

Nahum: Means "consolation."

Habakkuk: Book of faith.

Zephaniah: Warns of coming judgment of God.

Haggai: Sent to awaken the people.

Zechariah: Concerned with sin and moral decay of people.

Malachi: Sovereignty of God.

New Testament

Matthew: Instruction of new Christians.

Mark: Jesus as "Son of God."

Luke: Jesus as Savior.

John: The miracles of Jesus as signs.

Acts: The Holy Spirit.

Romans: Main truth of gospel to those in Rome.

1 and 2 Corinthians: Message of sanctification.

Galatians: Salvation.

Ephesians: Church is the body and Christ is the Head.

Philippians: Letter of joy.

Colossians: Jesus as Lord and Redeemer.

1 and 2 Thessalonians: To encourage.

1 and 2 Timothy: Solemn charge.

Titus: Connects doctrine, faithful men and godly lives.

Philemon: Relationships between Christians.

Hebrews: To inform and encourage Christians.

James: Plea for vital Christianity.

1 and 2 Peter: To encourage and strengthen.

1, 2 and 3 John: Known as "apostle of love."

Jude: Rebukes false teachers.

Revelation: Book of prophecy.